I am going to try & make the world, by God's help better & brighter by my being here—

Bellingrath Gardens
and Home

A Pictorial Story in Color
"The Garden for All Seasons"

Near Mobile, Alabama

Published by The Bellingrath-Morse Foundation

There are few places in the world where the magic of rapturous beauty is still to be found. One is Bellingrath Gardens, on the Isle-aux-Oies River, near Mobile, Alabama.

Visitors entering this vast and lovely estate soon realize they have discovered a wonderland. Overhead, from branches of aged oaks, cascade graceful wisps of Spanish moss, and the sun-dappled, flower-bordered paths excite the eye with loveliness. Man and Nature have harmoniously combined efforts to fashion a magnificent garden. The trail that winds so casually through the whispering pines is frequently enhanced by an artful vista that delightfully blends with the natural surroundings.

One of the charms of Bellingrath Gardens is that it is truly "The Garden for All Seasons." Mr. Bellingrath was fond of comparing his beloved "Charm Spot of the Deep South" to a lovely lady with 52 gowns, one for each week of the year. The metaphor suggests the constantly changing beauty of the Gardens, ever enchanting, never the same.

The new year greets the continuing exquisite beauty of camellias, more than 4,000 of them in hundreds of varieties; and azaleas are ablaze with color usually in February-March, with more than 250,000 plants in spectacular bloom. February also is the time when the Gardens are blanketed by more than 100,000 multi-colored tulips, hyacinths, daffodils and freesia. Roses appear in profusion from April to late October; and from April to September a variety of brilliant foliage plants and flowers, including mountain laurel, dogwood, salvia, caladium, allamanda, hydrangea and gardenia, brightly decorate the Gardens. In October-November, more than 60,000 plants of chrysanthemums, with millions of blooms, create the world's largest outdoor display of mums. And the year is closed with brilliant poinsettias of all shades during early December.

Comments from the many thousands of visitors who tour the Gardens each year are extravagant with praise. Whatever facet of this many-splendored place appeals most to the individual visitor, all share a common experience: the quiet, peaceful and tranquil atmosphere gives one a feeling of reverence and of closer communion with the one Creator of all beauty.

Facing Page—Autumn, a favorite season of the year for visitors, is the theme of this setting in the Entrance Mall.

Left—Designed to resemble the Rotary Club emblem, the Rose Garden is in bloom approximately 9 months of the year.
Bottom—Iron gates, which once welcomed guests to a Louisiana ante-bellum plantation, are near the entrance to the Gardens.

Many colorful varieties of the very popular rose may be enjoyed in this beautiful setting including the Peace Rose with its delicate colors. Tropical water lilies also add beauty to the Rose Garden. Overlooking the Rose Garden is a bridge of iron lacework and old hand-made brick.

Facing Page — **Top** — The Great Lawn, with its expanse of green grass, is bordered in late fall by a massive display of chrysanthemums and cassias. **Bottom**—One of several small gardens with palms, hexagonal flagstones, a mini-lawn and seasonal flowers.

Left—The Conservatory is home to bromeliads, orchids and many other exotic plants.

Facing Page—Left—Giant yellow hibiscus. **Right**—An azalea tree against the deep blue of a late winter/early spring sky. **Bottom**—Golden yellow allamandas with rich green foliage border the Great Lawn.

Left—Venerable live oaks, with Spanish Moss, frame the Bellingrath Home, as brightly colored tulips add color to this Deep South setting.

A massive display of tulips enhances the beauty of this pathway leading to one of the many pools that reflect lovely flowers around its borders.

Facing Page—Top—Two views of a mermaid who reigns elegantly over her corner of the Garden. **Bottom**—An ancient live oak tree, with its lacy Spanish moss, overhangs cinerarias, Easter lilies and amaryllis.

The Biblical story of Rebecca-at-the-Well is told on this hand-some bronze plaque at the head of a flower-bordered fountain.

The trumpet-like bloom of the azalea has its own individual beauty or may be used in mass displays with other flowers.

Facing Page—Flower-banked pool with fountains playing on the water, and as "The flowers appear on the earth; the time of the singing birds is come..." Song of Solomon 2:12.

Preceding Pages—The Christmas Season is greeted with the festive foliage of poinsettias, and early springtime features Snow azaleas around a portion of the South Terrace adjacent to one of several balconies of the Bellingrath Home. The tiny flowers at top right are ageratum.

Left and Right—Various views of the Bellingrath Grotto overlooking the Isle-aux-Oies River and a spacious wharf where boats land from nearby resorts and guests disembark.

Facing Page—Proud amaryllis stand with heads held high and also decorate a restful spot on the front terrace of the Home, while squirrels scamper throughout the Gardens.

Left—The petunia gives the appearance of a rare and exotic plant. **Center**—An agapanthus. **Bottom**—Tropical water lilies share the sunlight in front of the Home.

The unusual chenille plant, a tree full of mums and a close-up of allamandas show their lush growth and beautiful coloring.

Facing Page—Patio of the Bellingrath Home and its view of the South Terrace and Great Lawn.

The Bellingrath Home

Few residences anywhere combine the charm of design and construction, the richness of furnishings and the rarity of objets d'art that are to be found in The Bellingrath Home.

The furniture, the old English silver, the fabulous collection of china and rare porcelain are known as The Bessie Morse Bellingrath Collection in memory of Mrs. Bellingrath who painstakingly gathered these priceless objects from all over the world.

The house itself, built in 1935, is of handmade brick and wrought-iron lacework, all over a century old. In the words of the late George B. Rogers, the architect who designed it, the house is "a mingling of the French, English and Mediterranean influences, while the interior represents a blend of decor embracing chiefly the English Renaissance and Colonial America." As handsome as is the exterior of the Home, visitors are still not prepared for the magnificence to be found within.

Here is a comprehensive collection of antique furniture, including French and English pieces that reflect both the Victorian and latter-day French influences. Complementing the furniture are rare 18th and 19th Century pieces of Meissen (Dresden), Sevres and English porcelains. Four different sets of 22-carat gold overlay service plates, one set painted and signed by Angelica Kaufman (c. 1741-1807), are to be seen as well as nine complete dinner services and an exquisite collection of antique silver.

After Mrs. Bellingrath died in 1943, Mr. Bellingrath continued to live in the Home in the center of his beloved Gardens until the time of his death in 1955. It was then opened to the public, according to his wishes, by the non-profit charitable foundation which he had established in 1950.

Facing Page—A priceless Meissen (Dresden) urn, c. late 1700s.

Left—Drawing Room of the Bellingrath Home with its many interesting period furnishings, including a French porcelain clock and urns by Jacob Petite, c. 1790, on the Adam-type mantel. The gold leaf mirror is Louis XVI.

Elegance is the word for the Main Dining Room of the Home. Many visitors have said this is the most beautiful room they have seen in America. The rare centerpiece is of Meissen porcelain and ormolu.

English Chippendale dining table and chairs formerly owned by Sir Thomas Lipton. The Aubusson tapestry rug is of the Louis XVI period, c. 1774. The hand carved rosewood console table made for Princess Louise, grandmother of Kaiser Wilhelm II, is in the upstairs hall.

Facing Page—A Louis XV porcelain urn (Sevres) and a family group in French bisque is one of several hundred porcelain figures in the Home. A guest bedroom displays the exquisite detail in which Mrs. Bellingrath furnished her home.

Right—A corner of the upstairs Morning Room and, below, a hand-carved four-poster bed in a guest bedroom.

The porcelain group is 18th century Meissen.

Facing Page—Mrs. Bellingrath's bedroom with its hand-carved bed by Mallard, c. 1860, and Mr. Bellingrath's Jacobean-style oak desk inlaid in ivory and mother-of-pearl.

This small dining room contains many interesting pieces from various countries, and in the pantry and kitchen areas is the Bellingrath collection of rare silver, china and glassware. The bust is of English bisque by Copeland.

The silver collection of English and French sterling is regarded by many as one of America's greatest.

Facing Page—Porch Dining Room with portraits of Generals Washington, Lee and Jackson in needle point and petit point. Also pictured is a kitchen corner with a table of Alabama marble. On the porch is an unusual Oriental hand-carved mahogany table.

After viewing the works of the finest craftsmen of Europe and America, visitors return to the out-of-doors beauty of Bellingrath Gardens. Having seen so much, one finds it difficult to believe that still further surprises in loveliness lie ahead. They are soon evident, however, along the flagstone paths with new vistas and scenes that challenge the imagination.

The Works of
EDWARD MARSHALL BOEHM

The Bellingrath Gallery of Boehm Porcelain is located in a building that once served as a guest house and garage adjacent to the Bellingrath Home. It provides a perfect place for the visitor to relax and enjoy the world's greatest porcelain sculptures. These contemporary pieces are the work of Edward Marshall Boehm (1913-1969) of Trenton, New Jersey.

When Mr. Boehm died, he left a heritage of artistry in a medium that originated in the ancient lands of China but had never before been so perfected. His talents and influence were of such magnitude that his wife and the artists he had gathered together have been able to carry on the great work he began.

Mr. O. H. Delchamps, Sr., a businessman and philanthropist of Mobile, Alabama, was one of Mr. Boehm's early admirers. The genuine respect the two men had for each other soon developed into a deep and lasting personal friendship. On March 9, 1967, in a dedication ceremony attended by patrons of the art from as far away as England, Mr. and Mrs. O. H. Delchamps, Sr., Mr. and Mrs. A. F. Delchamps, Sr., and Mrs. Annie Delchamps Moore, all of Mobile, presented a collection of 86 pieces to The Bellingrath-Morse Foundation. Mr. and Mrs. Boehm presented the large Ivory-billed Woodpeckers. Since that time many more pieces have been added.

Visitors to the Gardens are directed through the Boehm Gallery and encouraged to pause and enjoy these replicas of some of Nature's most beautiful creations.

The Bellingrath Gallery of Boehm Porcelain is the world's largest collection of porcelain birds sculptured by Edward Marshall Boehm open to the public.

The Ivory Billed Woodpeckers, over seven feet tall on its plinth, is believed to be the largest hard-paste porcelain sculpture ever made. It was created for a special Boehm showing held in London in 1964. This masterpiece, some five months in the making, is in the center of the Boehm Gallery.

Above—Song Sparrows with tulips. **Right**—Wood Thrushes with azaleas.

Facing Page—A male Crested Flycatcher in the autumnal setting of a sweet gum tree.

Above—Western Bluebirds with yellow wild azaleas. **Right** — Ptarmigan, with feathered feet and legs, in winter plumage.

Varied Buntings in a setting of
"Fritillaria imperialis" or
"Crown Imperial" of the Lily family.

Philodendron, ferns, and orchids
provide the setting for a pair of
Yellow-winged Sugarbirds and a pair
of Purple Sugarbirds.

The protective
instincts of the Blue
Jay are depicted as
the female feeds her
young and the male
rails at a chameleon.

Right—The Chinese Bamboo is the Gardens' fastest grower, reaching full height in about a month during early spring. **Below**—View across Mirror Lake toward the Bellingrath Gallery of Boehm Porcelain.

THE NORTH BAYOU

An observation platform is equipped with free binoculars so the visitor can get a close look at the inhabitants of a typical southern bayou and environs.

It's a world of its own and includes deer, ducks, many kinds of birdlife, armadillos, geese, otters, raccoon, opossums, beavers, muskrat, turtles, nutria, alligators, shrimp, crabs, snails, fish . . . the list could go on and on. Some of these creatures are nocturnal and others are well camouflaged. Most are elusive but they are all there for the patient and close observer to see.

Bellingrath Gardens has several large undisturbed areas in its total property that provide a natural habitat for many kinds of wildlife.

Facing Page—From inside a Summer House, a walk leads to the Camellia Arboretum of more than a thousand varieties of camellias, including the Mathotiana Supreme shown here.

Two opposite views of Mirror Lake with fall foliage

Facing Page—Swans add to the interest of Mirror Lake and seem to enjoy posing, except when nesting, for visitors' cameras.

Left—Lilium alba. Center Left—Mountain laurel. Center Top—Rothschild Supreme hybrid azalea. Below—A Monarch butterfly with daisies. Vivid reflections on Mirror Lake are responsible for its name.

Facing Page—The rustic bridge spanning one end of Mirror Lake and the Rockery leading from the lake. The Rockery was built under the supervision of Mrs. Bellingrath who directed the placement of each stone.

Left—A view from the Summer House adjacent to the Camellia Arboretum.

Below—A begonia on moss-covered stone, ferns and the sound of falling water add to the charm of the Rockery.

Left—Entrance to the Oriental-American Garden where two cultures are blended to create unusual beauty completely different from the rest of Bellingrath Gardens.

Below—A colorful candlestick tree and a cardinal "sit" for their portraits.

The picturesque, exotic beauty of the Oriental-American Garden is shown in these six views.

Cascading chrysanthemums accent this beautiful
and tranquil scene in the Oriental-American Garden.

Ducks and swans, as well as flamingos, find sanctuary in the Oriental-American Garden, as do nearly 200 species of other birds which either make their home in Bellingrath Gardens or visit during their migrations.

During early 1977, snow fell heavily on Bellingrath Gardens. The rising sun melted it during the early morning hours but not before the camera captured these unforgettable scenes. The snow was one of Nature's phenomenons that rarely occurs and even the flamingos were none the worse for it, and plants benefited from the unusual weather.

Below—The Rose Garden becomes a showplace for tulips—32,000 of them—during the late winter months.

These two delicate water colors
by Mrs. Louise Estes of Mobile
show the different stages of
growth of a Peace Rose and a
Betty Sheffield Supreme Camellia from bud to exquisite flower.

WALTER DUNCAN BELLINGRATH
1869-1955

BESSIE MORSE BELLINGRATH
1878-1943

Founders of Bellingrath Gardens

Born in Atlanta, Georgia, Walter D. Bellingrath began his career at the age of 17 as a railroad station agent and telegraph operator for the Louisville and Nashville Railroad in the small Alabama town of Castleberry. At the time of his death at 86, he had become one of the South's great leaders in business, church, educational and civic affairs. He moved to Mobile in 1903 and founded the Coca-Cola Bottling Company in that city. He later married Bessie Mae Morse of Mobile, whose tireless energy and love of beauty played a predominant part in the masterpiece of their life's work: the creation of Bellingrath Gardens and the establishment of The Bessie Morse Bellingrath Collection of antique furniture, Old English silver, rare porcelains and fine china.

Walter D. Bellingrath
in his beloved Garden.

History of Bellingrath Gardens

This early painting shows the rustic site of now fabulous Bellingrath Gardens, which began as a fishing lodge in 1917 for Walter D. and Bessie Morse Bellingrath. It was Mrs. Bellingrath who first began planting azaleas in the woods around the lodge. So successful were her efforts that she and her husband soon became enthusiastic over the possibility of creating a wondrously beautiful garden from the forest around them.

In 1927, on a trip to Europe, the Bellingraths were enormously impressed by the great gardens they found there. They decided to call upon professional landscape architects to help them in their labor of love on the Isle-aux-Oies River. The aid of George B. Rogers, internationally known landscape designer and architect, was enlisted and the major aspects of the transformation were begun.

Not until 1932 were the Gardens opened to the public. The response to the Bellingrath's invitation to come see their gardens was so overwhelming that the Sheriff's office was called to help untangle the traffic snarl. To help with the tremendous cost of upkeep, it was decided that an admission fee must be charged. This has been customary ever since.

The Gardens grew in size as additional acres of woodlands surrounding them were landscaped and planted. One of the interesting developments is the Camellia Arboretum, which is intended to provide the camellia enthusiast an opportunity to compare the growing and flowering habits of the many, many varieties of this queen of all flowers. This is perhaps the most complete collection of its kind in the world.

Both Mr. and Mrs. Bellingrath had the satisfaction of seeing their fondest dream become a reality in the unsurpassed beauty of Bellingrath Gardens. Had they been buried in the Gardens instead of in the family plot in Magnolia Cemetery in Mobile, their epitaph might well have been copied from Sir Christopher Wren's in St. Paul's Cathedral, which he designed: "If you seek a monument, look about you."

The Bellingrath-Morse Foundation

The purpose of the Bellingrath-Morse Foundation is best explained in Mr. Bellingrath's own words as written in the preamble to the Deed of Trust creating the Foundation on February 1, 1950.

"In the evening of our lives my beloved wife, Bessie Morse Bellingrath, and I found untold pleasure and happiness in the development of the Gardens which bear our name. During the past decade thousands of our fellow citizens have enjoyed the rare and lovely spectacle which nature, with our help, has provided in this 'Charm Spot of the Deep South.' The inspiration which we received as we carried on our work of developing the Gardens and the pleasant and appreciative reaction of the many visitors to the Gardens resulted in plans for the perpetuation of this beauty, so that those who come after us may visit the Gardens and enjoy them. In working out our plans, it occurred to us that the operation of the Gardens could be carried on in a way that would continue their existence and yet fulfill another worthy objective of ours. To this end, I am providing herein that the income from the operations of the Gardens be devoted to the intellectual and religious upbuilding of young men and women, as well as to foster and perpetuate those Christian values which were recognized by our forefathers as essential for the building of a great nation."

Mr. Bellingrath died on August 8, 1955, leaving the bulk of his estate, including the Coca-Cola Bottling Company, Inc., of Mobile to the Foundation. Today the Gardens are under the administration of the Trustees of The Bellingrath-Morse Foundation. The Corporate Trustee is the First National Bank of Mobile, of which Mr. Bellingrath was a director. The individual trustees are men who, over a period of time, were closely associated with Mr. Bellingrath.

With the establishment of The Bellingrath-Morse Foundation, Southwestern at Memphis, Huntingdon College at Montgomery, and Stillman College at Tuscaloosa became beneficiaries along with the Central Presbyterian Church of Mobile (as a perpetual memorial to his parents), and the St. Francis Street Methodist Church of Mobile (as a perpetual memorial to his wife's parents).

It is incumbent upon the colleges, in order to qualify as a beneficiary, that each student shall be required to take a Bible course. Thus, through the Foundation, Mr. Bellingrath is carrying out a long fostered and cherished plan of perpetuating world famed Bellingrath Gardens and, at the same time, providing long term benefits to the colleges which carry on in the Christian tradition.

NORTH BAYOU

ISLE-AUX-OIES (Fowl) RIVER

Entrance to the
BELLINGRATH
HOME

MIRROR
LAKE

CAMELLIA
ARBORETUM

GREAT LAWN

ORIENTAL-AMERICAN
GARDEN

PET MOTEL

SERVICE ROAD

ENTRANCE
BUILDING

Bellingrath
Gallery,
Gift Shop,
Lounges and
Restaurant

PARKING
AREA

1 Entrance to the Gardens
2 Rose Garden (Rotary Club
   Emblem)
3 Exotica Conservatory
4 Brick Patio
5 Camellia Parterre
6 Pool — Mermaid
7 Pool — Rebecca at the Well
8 Monolith — History of the
   Gardens
9 South Terrace
10 Grotto
11 Wharf
12 North Terrace
13 Entrance to the Bellingrath
   Home
14 Boehm Porcelain Sculptures —
   and Rest Rooms
15 Mirror Lake Terrace
16 North Bayou Observation
   Tower
17 Summer House — Camellia
   Arboretum Entrance and Exit
18 Mirror Lake and Rockery Vista
19 Bubbling Pool
20 Rustic Bridge Across
   Mirror Lake
21 Rockery
22 Label Garden
23 Oriental-American Garden
   Entrance and Exit
24 Exit from the Gardens